The Story of *Titanic's*
CHAIRMAN ISMAY

BY MOLLY JONES

Published by The Child's World®
1980 Lookout Drive • Mankato, MN 56003-1705
800-599-READ • www.childsworld.com

Acknowledgments
The Child's World®: Mary Berendes, Publishing Director
Red Line Editorial: Design, editorial direction, and production
Photographs ©: Underwood & Underwood/Corbis, cover, 1; AP Images, 4; Bain News
Service/Library of Congress, 6, 17; Everett Historical/Shutterstock Images, 8; Ralph
White/Corbis, 10, 14; Underwood & Underwood/Library of Congress, 12; Harris and
Ewing/Library of Congress, 18; Bettmann/Corbis, 21

ISBN 9781634074636

LCCN 2015946309

Printed in the United States of America
Mankato, MN
December, 2015
PA02287

ABOUT THE AUTHOR

Molly Jones has a PhD in educational research. She has taught at the high
school, college, and graduate levels. Her books for young readers are
about history, political issues, and health. She lives on Lake Murray in South
Carolina and enjoys reading, sailing, and yoga.

Table of
CONTENTS

Chapter 1

THE GRANDEST SHIP

It was the morning of Wednesday, April 10, 1912. J. Bruce Ismay had arrived at the dock in Southampton, England. He gazed up at the marvelous *Titanic*. It was the world's largest steamship. That day, the grand ship was preparing for its first voyage. Ismay excitedly boarded the vessel.

For Ismay, it was a day of celebration. He was the **chairman** of White Star Line, the company that owned the *Titanic*. The magnificent ship was very popular. More than 1,000 people had bought tickets for its first voyage. The *Titanic* offered luxury for wealthy passengers. Cheaper tickets were available for second- and third-class passengers. The ship was set to make big profits for Ismay and his company.

Newspaper reporters had published stories about the great ship. On that morning, crowds gathered to peek at the grand vessel. Passengers began boarding the ship at 9:30 a.m. As they arrived, reporters snapped pictures.

At noon, the *Titanic* departed from Southampton. The ship would stop twice to pick up passengers. Then it would steam across the Atlantic Ocean to New York. A total of 2,223 passengers and crew members were taking the trip.

Five years earlier, the great ship had been only a dream. Ismay had discussed the idea with others in the shipping industry. But no pier or dock was large enough to hold his planned ship. Finally, a wealthy shipyard owner named Lord William Pirrie offered to help. Pirrie hired workers to construct a dock large enough for the ship. It was the largest dock ever built. Then Ismay and Pirrie planned to create the largest, most luxurious ship on Earth.

The *Titanic* took two years to build. Its construction was completed by 3,000 men. The finished ship was nearly as long as three soccer fields. It was 11 stories high. Four smokestacks, or funnels, added to that height. Each rose 62 feet (19 m) and measured 22 feet (7 m) across.

▲ **Crews worked to construct the *Titanic* (left) and the *Olympic*, another White Star Line ship.**

The chairman had spent years planning for the ship's first voyage. But on that day, he was on the ship as a regular first-class passenger. He could relax and enjoy the journey. Ismay's elegant quarters had two bedrooms, a bathroom, and a private **promenade** deck. The rooms featured handsome furniture, including armchairs, a long table, and a fake fireplace.

Other ships at the time were often slow and cramped. Passengers were used to long, uncomfortable journeys. The *Titanic*, however, was designed for pleasure. A first-class passenger wrote that the ship was "huge," with furniture "in the best of taste."[1] A **wireless** was another luxury. Passengers enjoyed sending messages to people on shore. Soon, the wireless room was bustling with activity. Operators hurried to place and receive all of the messages.

The ship had a crew of 897 workers. More than 150 firemen shoveled coal to power the ship. Up above, chefs prepared delicious meals. A first-class dinner menu might offer 20 to 30 choices. Breakfast was just as plentiful. Even third-class options were better than those on most other ships.

Ismay took pride in the ship's luxury and its safety. The builders had constructed 15 watertight **bulkheads** in the body of the ship. If a collision pierced one bulkhead, others would still keep water out. In case of an emergency, crew members could

▲ The *Titanic*'s features included a grand reception room for first-class passengers.

use the wireless. Messages from other ships would alert them to dangerous conditions ahead.

Ismay was confident that the *Titanic* would not sink. As a result, he did not worry much about certain safety features. The boat deck stowed 20 lifeboats. Each lifeboat could hold about 65 people. That was slightly more than British ship regulations required. But it was not enough for all of the passengers on board. Ismay believed that lifeboats would never be needed.

The chairman also trusted the captain to run the *Titanic* safely. Edward Smith was a white-haired man who had been on the seas for 43 years. As captain of eight major ships before the *Titanic*, Smith was highly regarded by his crew members. Passengers were also fond of him. "We all felt so safe with him," one passenger wrote. "One knew how deeply he felt the responsibility of his ship and all on board."[2]

As the ship set off, the captain and his crew saved the *Titanic* from a possible disaster. The large ship churned up water, breaking the ropes of a smaller ship nearby. The smaller ship began to drift toward the *Titanic*. The two ships nearly collided. But the *Titanic*'s crew ably maneuvered the vessel away from the smaller ship. The near-collision did not alarm Ismay. He believed that the captain and the ship could cope with dangers at sea.

Chapter 2

ICEBERG AHEAD

On Friday, April 12, crew members became aware of a new danger. Other ships began to send messages to the *Titanic*. They warned of icebergs in the *Titanic*'s path. A collision with an iceberg could badly damage a ship, especially if the ship was traveling fast. Despite the dangers, the *Titanic* sailed smoothly on Friday and Saturday. Each night, Chairman Ismay dined in the ship's first-class restaurant. Sometimes he chatted with the ship's officers. None of them mentioned dangers the ship faced.

On the morning of Sunday, April 14, Ismay visited the **bridge** of the ship. The crew had continued to receive warning messages about ice. The captain gave Ismay one of the messages. Ismay read it and put it in his pocket. Later that day, he shared the message with other passengers. To Ismay, the message simply reminded him of the ship's safety. Surely the *Titanic*'s sturdy construction could protect it from dangers.

Some of the warning messages may not have reached the crew. Ever since the *Titanic* set off, the two wireless operators had been busy. This day was no exception. They received and delivered messages to and from shore and other ships. Messages came for Ismay, Captain Smith, other officers, and passengers. For Ismay, having wireless devices on board was paying off. Wealthy passengers paid to send messages to friends and family on shore. But the wireless office did not have a large enough staff. While one operator slept, the other could not handle all of the messages. Some warning messages probably never got to the bridge where officers could read them.

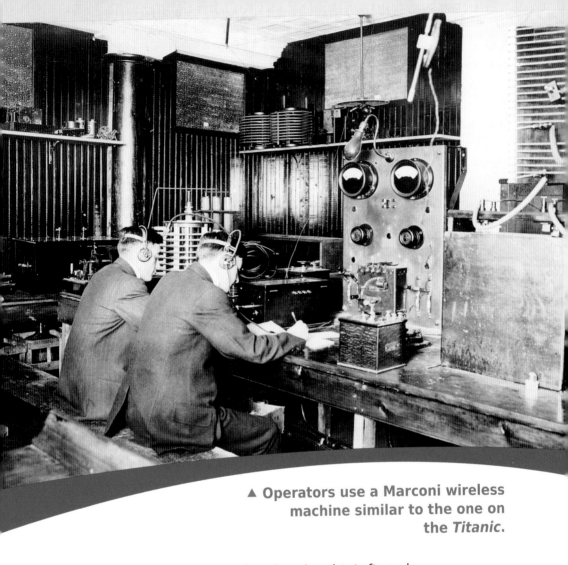

▲ Operators use a Marconi wireless machine similar to the one on the *Titanic*.

That night, Ismay again dined in the ship's first-class restaurant. He was in a happy mood as he shared a meal with the ship's doctor. The *Titanic* had been sailing at a fast speed of around 22 knots. Ismay announced proudly that the ship might set a speed record. After a pleasant meal, the chairman retired to bed. The ocean was calm. The sky was pitch-dark with just a few stars shining.

While Ismay slept, everything changed. At about 11:40 p.m., a *Titanic* lookout spotted an iceberg directly ahead of the **bow**. Quickly, the officer at the wheel changed the ship's course. But it was too late. The lookout heard a large scraping sound. The *Titanic* had collided with the iceberg. It ripped a large gash into the side of the ship. Water poured in. The bulkheads could not stop the surging water from flooding the ship.

Ismay woke with a start. He felt the jarring movements of the ship. The chairman pulled on a coat and pair of trousers over his pajamas. He met Captain Smith on the ship's bridge. "Do you think the ship is seriously damaged?" Ismay asked.

"I'm afraid she is," Smith replied.[3] He ordered the crew to prepare lifeboats and begin loading passengers.

The *Titanic* was not unsinkable. Ismay knew his ship was doomed.

Chapter 3

TERROR AT SEA

Crew members began to knock on passengers' doors. "Gather your lifejackets and come to the deck," said the **stewards**.[4] Chairman Ismay returned to his room for a few minutes. But shortly after midnight, he was back on the bridge. Ismay began assisting crew members with the lifeboats.

Captain Smith ordered that distress signals be sent to alert nearby ships. The ship set off rockets to get the attention of other ships' crews. At 12:05 a.m., the _Titanic_ sent a message to all ships in the area. It said, "Position 41.46 N 50.14 W. Require assistance. Struck iceberg."[5]

The ship began to lean. The deck was flooded. A sea tradition said that women and children should board the lifeboats first. For an hour and a half, Ismay helped gather passengers to board the boats. Crew members turned away some men from the lifeboats. Officers lowered lifeboats into the ocean.

The crew had not practiced what to do if the ship sank. In some parts of the ship, people crowded around the lifeboats. Not everyone got a seat. Other lifeboats left with empty seats.

Collapsible Boat C was one of the last lifeboats. When it was being loaded, Ismay saw that there were still seats available. No more women and children were waiting nearby. Ismay later said that he believed the ship was empty. But he was wrong. Ismay jumped into the boat. Thirty minutes later, as passengers rowed the boat away to safety, the **stern** of the _Titanic_ rose high in the air. Many passengers and crew members were still on the ship. Then, bow first, the great ship sank to the bottom of the Atlantic Ocean. Ismay could not bear to look back at the ship and its passengers. "I did not wish to see her go down," he later said. "I am glad I did not."[6]

For hours, the lifeboats drifted. Ismay and the other passengers shivered in the cold. At 4:00 a.m., a ship came near. The *Carpathia* had seen the *Titanic*'s distress signals. Crew members on the *Carpathia* began hauling the *Titanic* survivors aboard.

On the *Carpathia*, Ismay had the sad task of informing White Star Line of the disaster. "Deeply regret to advise you," his telegram said, "*Titanic* sank this morning [April] fifteenth after collision with iceberg. Serious loss of life. Further particulars later."[7]

There were 706 people who survived the sinking of the *Titanic*. The disaster claimed the lives of 1,517 people. Most crew members, including Captain Smith, died. Many factors contributed to the tragedy. The warning messages from the wireless did not reach all the crew members. Ship officers did not realize how serious the ice situation was.

Ismay's confidence in the ship's safety also added to the risk. With only 20 lifeboats on board, hundreds of people did not have seats. The crew had practiced lowering and raising two lifeboats, but no other lifeboat **drill** had been held. The ship had begun to sink before all the boats were ready. Some boats were not even

▲ Crew members on the *Carpathia* rescued the survivors from the *Titanic*.

used. Others, such as the one Ismay boarded, were launched before they were full. If all lifeboats had been completely filled, 400 more people might have survived.

Ismay was given a private cabin on the *Carpathia*. Many other *Titanic* survivors slept on tables or the floor. One woman claimed that Ismay said, "I'm Ismay! Give me a stateroom at once."[8] Passengers began to talk about Ismay's behavior. Some blamed him for the sinking of the ship.

Chapter 4

GUILT AND BLAME

On April 18, three days after the *Titanic* sank, the *Carpathia* arrived in New York. On board were the 706 *Titanic* survivors. Bruce Ismay was among them. Ismay had been in a state of shock those three days. He sat silent and alone in his cabin. Some other passengers wondered why he shut himself away.

Americans had heard about the *Titanic* disaster. Crowds came to see the *Carpathia* when it arrived. They wondered how such a tragedy could happen. The very next day, the U.S. Senate began an **inquiry**. Senators questioned passengers and crew. They wanted to know how the collision happened and why so many people had died. Ismay was the first person they questioned.

Some senators treated Ismay harshly. They believed he had not cared enough about passengers' safety. Senators asked for information about lifeboats and other equipment on the ship. They also wanted to know if the *Titanic* had conducted safety drills.

Senators released their final report on May 28, 1912. They did not find Ismay responsible for the disaster. The White Star Line had followed the British rules for ship safety. The *Titanic* had more lifeboats than the regulations required. However, these rules had been formed before ships as large as the *Titanic* existed. The senators suggested new rules for ships in the United States and elsewhere. The new rules would make sure that ships carried enough lifeboats for all passengers.

Ismay also faced criticism from the public. Newspaper reporters asked why Ismay survived when so many passengers died. A reporter for the *New York American* wrote, "Mr. Ismay cares for nobody but himself. He leaves his ship to sink with its precious cargo of lives and does not care to lift his eyes."[9] Rumors swirled about Ismay. Some passengers said he knowingly left women and children behind on the *Titanic*. Others said he refused to help row his lifeboat to safety. Ismay described his actions differently. We may never know the full truth about how he acted when the *Titanic* sank.

In New York, Ismay defended himself for boarding a lifeboat while other passengers went down with the ship. "I was calling for the women and children to come in," he said. "I had been helping women and children into the boat. I was standing by the boat. I helped everybody that was there. As the boat was being lowered away, I got in."[10] Ismay also said he was on the *Titanic* as a passenger. Even though his company owned the ship, he did not have the responsibilities of a crew member. Still, many were unconvinced. They believed Ismay could have done more to help other passengers.

Many in England were kinder to Ismay. After the Senate inquiry, he returned to his home in Liverpool, England. A headline in the *Daily Sketch*, a British newspaper, read, "Mr. Bruce Ismay Welcomed Home with Cheers."[11]

Should Ismay have stayed on the ship and done more to help other passengers? Or was he right to board a lifeboat? For the rest of his life, Ismay was haunted by those questions. In 1916, he resigned from the White Star Line. "I never want to see a ship again, and I loved them so much," he wrote to a friend.[12] His wife, Florence, forbade others to mention the *Titanic* to Ismay. Ismay lived until 1937, but he stayed away from the public. The disaster had forever changed him.

▲ **At the inquiry, Ismay answered questions from senators.**

GLOSSARY

bow (BAU): The bow is the front part of a ship or boat. Passengers watched the waves from the bow.

bridge (BRIJ): The bridge is a raised area from which a ship is operated. The captain steered the ship from the bridge.

bulkheads (BULK-heds): Bulkheads are safety structures built into the body of a ship. The bulkheads keep water out of the ship.

chairman (CHAIR-mun): A chairman is a president of a company or group. J. Bruce Ismay was the chairman of White Star Line.

drill (DRIL): A drill is an exercise to learn or practice a skill. A captain can conduct a lifeboat drill so that officers learn safety rules.

inquiry (in-KWUH-ree): An inquiry is an official investigation. The U.S. Senate held an inquiry on the *Titanic* disaster.

promenade (PRAH-muh-nahd): A promenade is an area where passengers walk on a ship. Passengers strolled on the promenade.

stern (STURN): The stern is the rear part of a ship. The stern was the last part of the *Titanic* to sink.

stewards (STOO-urds): Stewards are helpers who take care of passengers on ships. Stewards helped passengers board the lifeboats.

wireless (WIRE-les): A wireless is a device for sending messages using radio waves. *Titanic* passengers used the wireless to send messages to the shore.

SOURCE NOTES

1. Nick Barratt. *Lost Voices from the Titanic*. New York: Palgrave McMillan, 2012. Print. 75.

2. Stephanie Barczewski. *Titanic: A Night Remembered*. London: Hambledon and London, 2004. Print. 164.

3. Ibid. 16.

4. Ibid. 20.

5. Michael Hughes and Katherine Bosworth, eds. *Titanic Calling: Wireless Communication During the Great Disaster*. Oxford: Bodleian Library, 2012. Print. 31.

6. "Testimony of J. Bruce Ismay." *United States Senate Inquiry*. Titanic Inquiry Project, n.d. Web. 20 June 2015.

7. "'Titanic Sank This Morning': Telegrams Sent by Shipping Firm's Head to HQ after He Was Plucked to Safety Are Revealed." *Daily Mail*. Associated Newspapers Ltd., 9 December 2011. Web. 7 May 2015.

8. "Woman Accuses Ismay." *The New York Times*. The New York Times Company, 22 April 1912. Web. 7 July 2015.

9. Stephanie Barczewski. *Titanic: A Night Remembered*. London: Hambledon and London, 2004. Print. 100.

10. Frances Wilson. *How to Survive the Titanic: The Sinking of J. Bruce Ismay*. New York: Harper Collins. Print. 253.

11. Paul Louden-Brown. "Ismay and the Titanic." *The Titanic Historical Society*. The Titanic Historical Society, Inc., 2014. Web. 7 July 2015.

12. Ibid.

TO LEARN MORE

Books

McDonnell, Vincent. *Titanic Tragedy*. Wilton, Ireland: Collins Press, 2007.

McPherson, Stephanie Sammartino. *Iceberg Right Ahead! The Tragedy of the Titanic*. Minneapolis, MN: Twenty-First Century Books, 2012.

Stewart, Melissa. *Titanic*. Washington, DC: National Geographic, 2012.

Web Sites

Visit our Web site for links about Chairman Ismay: childsworld.com/links

Note to Parents, Teachers, and Librarians: We routinely verify our Web links to make sure they are safe and active sites. So encourage your readers to check them out!

INDEX

6/2016